CCSS **Genre** Realistic

Essential Question
What shapes a person's identity?

M000209305

Homesick for American Samoa

by Diana Noonan
illustrated by Stephen Templer

Chapter 1

An Invitation

When the invitation to his cousin's wedding came in the mail, the whole village was excited. Salesi, however, could think only about the extra chores it would mean for him. His cousin Elisapeta lived in Los Angeles. That was a long way from Salesi's home in American Samoa.

The invitation came with two airplane tickets. That meant his mom and dad would be going, and they'd probably be away for almost three weeks. He and his big brother, Pele, would have to take care of everything at home: the chickens, pigs, garden, house—not to mention Grandma!

For the next week, Salesi moped around the house. After school he didn't even feel like playing football or going fishing with his friends. He just sat on the porch, his chin resting on his hand.

It wasn't fair that there were only two plane tickets. There was so much to see in Los Angeles. His cousins from California had told him all about it on their visits to his village. It sounded like Pago Pago, the capital of American Samoa, but bigger and better. His cousins said there were some really cool amusement parks, too. They were so big you could spend the whole day there and still not have time to go on every ride!

There were even movie stars living in L.A.! Sometimes his cousins spotted stars sitting outside cafés downtown. There was also delicious food. Occasionally his cousins went out for breakfast. They said you could choose from 27 different kinds of fruit smoothies. Salesi didn't really believe that, but it made his mouth water all the same.

Suddenly a squawking chicken came out from under the porch. It raced across the yard with the neighbor's dog following behind it.

Then Salesi heard his mom calling him. She probably wanted him to get something from the store or gather some bananas from the garden. Or maybe his grandma wanted him to help her walk down to the beach. She liked to sit on the sand and talk to her old friends. Salesi sighed. He'd be doing a lot more of that kind of thing when his parents were in California.

"You've been daydreaming ever since you came home from school!" Salesi's mom said sharply when he walked inside. "If you don't do your jobs, you won't earn your allowance, and then you'll have no money to spend in L.A."

Salesi's mouth dropped. Then he saw his brother, Pele, leaning against the wall behind their mom, chuckling. The next minute, their father walked in. He was grinning and waving the invitations. Surely they couldn't be trying to tell him that … no … it was impossible!

"Yes, Salesi, you and I are going to Elisapeta's wedding!" exclaimed Pele.

"I need to stay here and take care of Grandma, and someone from the family has to go," explained their mom.

"And I'm not going without your mother, because I'd miss her cooking too much!" said their dad, laughing.

Salesi tried to speak, but all that came out of his mouth at first was a squeak of excitement. "Wow! I've only ever been to Pago Pago, and now I'm going to Los Angeles."

He shot out the door and down to the beach to find his friends. He couldn't wait to tell them the news. The only problem was that no one was going to believe him. He could hardly believe it himself!

Salesi's mom excitedly started getting presents ready for Salesi and Pele to take to their relatives. His dad was excited, too, but his grandmother looked sad as she quietly sat weaving Elisapeta's wedding present.

"Grandma has seen many of our relatives visit California and then move there," his mom whispered to Salesi. "She thinks you might want to do the same when you're older—leave American Samoa and forget about *fa'a Samoa*, the Samoan way of life."

"I'd never forget the Samoan way, even if I did move to a big city," replied Salesi.

"Perhaps you should tell her that," said his mom. "Although I'm not sure she'll believe you."

Chapter 2
L.A. Is Full of Fun

The flight to California seemed to take forever. Salesi and Pele talked about all the things they were going to see and do when they got there. When they arrived at the airport in L.A., three carloads of relatives were waiting to meet them there.

Salesi thought his aunts might suffocate him with all their hugs. Everyone kept asking questions about his home. Who had married whom? Did they have any children? When the car Salesi was riding in pulled in to the garage of a huge house, it was his turn to ask the questions.

"Where are we?" he asked his cousin Rylan. "I thought we were staying at your place."

"This is my place!" said Rylan, puzzled. "Come on, I'll show you your room."

Salesi slowly closed his gaping mouth. This enormous house was where his cousin lived!

Rylan took Salesi and Pele upstairs to a bedroom as big as Salesi's classroom back in Samoa. It had two double beds, two huge armchairs, and even its own bathroom!

Salesi performed a crazy little dance in front of a long mirror beside the shower. The mirror stretched all the way from the ceiling to the shiny white tiles on the floor. No wonder his grandmother was afraid he might not want to come home—this place was awesome!

"Hurry up, you two," called Aunt Vai. "We're going to Splash Out Fun."

"It's a water park, so expect to get drenched!" explained Rylan.

"Splash Out Fun only opened a month ago. Everything is new," said Aunt Vai once they were driving in the car.

Salesi looked out the car window. They were on a freeway with six lanes going in each direction. Tall palm trees waved down at them. An ambulance raced past with its lights flashing. Giant trucks rumbled past. In the sky, a helicopter buzzed and circled around.

Aunt Vai turned on some music, and Rylan started singing along to it. By the time they drove into the parking lot at Splash Out Fun, Salesi thought he was on another, very peculiar planet.

Every day for the rest of the week, a different cousin arrived to take Salesi and Pele somewhere exciting. One morning when they went out for breakfast, Salesi discovered it was true—you really *could* choose from 27 flavors of fruit smoothies!

"Hey, Pele, Salesi," said Uncle Aleni one afternoon. "Would you like to watch a 3-D movie?"

"How about coming to a basketball game with me tonight?" asked their cousin Telini.

By the end of the week, Salesi's head was spinning. He'd been on a rollercoaster and seen L.A. from the tallest building in the city. He'd visited a movie studio and been caught in rush-hour traffic on the freeway. It was all so amazing! When he and his cousins finally spotted a movie star sitting outside a cafe, Salesi wasn't even surprised.

There was one thing that Salesi did find strange, though. It was a weird feeling that crept up on him during his second week away from home. It started one night when he was watching TV. A commercial for a vacation on a Pacific island flashed onto the screen. Suddenly Salesi felt sad, or maybe he was just feeling a little lonely. It was hard to tell.

He snuggled further down into bed that night, but the mattress was too soft. He wished he could hear the sound of the ocean or even his dad snoring in the next room. In the morning, Salesi didn't feel like eating breakfast—not even bagels.

"You're not homesick, are you?" asked Aunt Vai in a teasing way.

Salesi shrugged. He didn't know what he felt. He'd never been away from home for more than a couple of nights, and his mom and dad had always been with him. He glanced at Pele to see how he was doing, but his brother seemed the same as ever.

"You've got the wedding to look forward to tomorrow," said Aunt Vai kindly. "That'll take your mind off things."

Chapter 3
Fa'a Samoa

Salesi woke up feeling miserable the morning of his cousin's wedding. It was a battle to open his eyes. He didn't want to get out of bed. On the other side of the room, Pele was fast asleep.

Salesi lay on his back and looked up at the wide ceiling. He wished he could hear the chatter of the parakeets that lived in the trees around his village. He wished he could just jump out of bed and run down to the beach for a fresh coconut. He'd like to run to his friend's house to see if he wanted to go fishing.

Most of all, he missed not being able to sneak into the kitchen and gobble up a spoonful of cold noodles from the refrigerator. He always did that in the morning before his mom woke up.

If only his mom, dad, and grandma had all been able to come to L.A.. A big, wet tear rolled out of the corner of Salesi's eye and onto the pillow. He couldn't let his cousins know how he felt. They'd think he was ungrateful for all the places they'd taken him. Salesi sniffed hard. As he did, he caught a familiar scent.

Salesi sat up in bed and pulled open the curtains. At first he thought he saw mist drifting past his window. Then he realized it was smoke. "Aunt Vai! Rylan!" he called, stumbling downstairs. "Help! Something's on fire. There's smoke coming from the yard!"

"Of course there's smoke!" grinned Aunt Vai. She peered out from behind a pile of vegetables that she was cutting up in the kitchen. "Uncle Leon has lit the *umu* for Elisapeta's wedding today. Remember?"

"Umu?" asked Salesi. "I thought we'd be going to a restaurant for the wedding breakfast. I didn't know you were making an umu like we do at home." He remembered the delicious flavor of food cooked in these ovens in the ground.

"Of course we're making an umu!" exclaimed Uncle Leon as he strode through the kitchen. "Today we're in American Samoa!"

By the time a bunch of his cousins arrived an hour later, Salesi's homesickness had almost disappeared. His cousins carried guitars and wore traditional Samoan clothing—*ta'ovala* and *lei*. Some of them carried plates of chop suey and cold chicken. He also spotted huge plates of corned beef, taro, and raw fish.

"This is exactly what we do in Samoa when there's a wedding," Salesi told his cousins. "How come you do this in L.A.? Who taught you how to make chop suey, Aunt Vai? How does Uncle Leon know how to make an umu?"

Salesi was so full of questions he almost forgot to give his cousin Elisapeta her presents from his parents and grandmother. He would never forget Elisapeta's reaction when she unwrapped the mat that his grandma had made for her.

She tore off the paper and then burst into tears. Suddenly it wasn't just cousin Elisapeta who was crying; it was most of his relatives. All his aunts and his female cousins and even some of the adult men were crying! Everyone started talking in Samoan as they admired the mat.

"What an amazing present!" exclaimed Elisapeta. "Only my grandmother weaves like this. The patterns that she uses express her individuality so well."

Elisapeta took the most beautiful flower from her bouquet and handed it to Salesi. "Would you please give this to Grandma?" she asked.

That afternoon Salesi ate and sang, and sang and ate. He watched the smoke from the umu drift up into the bright blue sky. When his aunt and uncle's neighbors arrived and sat on mats in the yard, he felt he really was back in his village.

That night Salesi went to bed feeling very tired. Before he went to sleep, he asked Aunt Vai if he could send an e-mail. He had something important to tell his grandma. It couldn't wait until he got home.

"Dear Grandmother," he typed. "Don't ever think that our relatives in California have forgotten their roots. The Samoan way is alive and well in L.A.."

He wrote to her about all the celebrations and how much everyone had admired the mat she had woven for Elisapeta. "And I'll tell you something else," typed Salesi. "L.A. is a fun place to visit, but I never want to live in a big city. I want to stay in American Samoa forever!"

Respond to Reading

Summarize

Use important details from *Homesick for American Samoa* to summarize the story. Your graphic organizer may help.

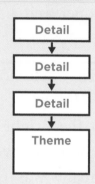

Text Evidence

1. How do you know that this story is realistic fiction? GENRE

2. What aspects of Samoan life help Salesi and his family celebrate their culture even when they are far away? THEME

3. On the morning of the wedding, Salesi finds it is "a battle to open his eyes." What does this metaphor mean? METAPHORS

4. Write about what Salesi learns about himself by the end of the story. How does this help communicate the story's theme?
WRITE ABOUT READING

Compare Texts

Read about the way a girl learns about herself
in a patchwork quilt.

Piecing It All Together

A Special Gift

On my tenth birthday, Aunt Telini
handed me a special quilt she'd made herself,
stitched from patches of familiar fabric,
wrapped in love, and tied with a ribbon
that shimmered like a butterfly in the sun.
"Untie the ribbon," she said.
"Let the quilt tell you who you are."

We spread the quilt across the floor.
So many colors, so many memories.

Memories

"This patch," said Aunt Telini,
"yellow as egg yolk, pink as frosting,
is from the apron I sewed for Cousin Esther.
Remember when she taught you how to bake?"
I remembered! Flour flying in the air,
more chocolate on my face than in the cake!
Now I love baking, just like she does!

"This patch is like the golfing pants
you made my dad!" I laughed.
Every Saturday when we played golf together,
I saw Dad wearing them!

"And this one here is from the shirt
you sewed for Uncle Tupe!"
Blue as the ocean, yellow as the Samoan sun.
I love my Uncle Tupe and his Samoan cooking.

Sewing My History

Aunt Telini and I carried the quilt to my room.
We flipped it up, and a family map,
a story, fell onto my bed.
Now every night, the quilt speaks to me
of all the people I love,
all the things I like to do.

I've begun making my own mini-quilt.
My favorite aunt, my sewing aunt,
is teaching me.
And guess what?
I love sewing, just like she does!

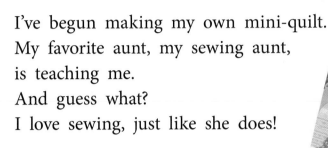

Make Connections

How can a quilt "tell you who you are"?
ESSENTIAL QUESTION

Compare Salesi in *Homesick for American Samoa* with
the narrator in the poem. What parts of Samoan life
are important to both of them? **TEXT TO TEXT**

Focus on Literary Elements

Alliteration People often think of alliteration as the opposite of rhyme. Rhyming words have the same ending sound, but alliterative words have the same beginning sound. Alliteration isn't just for poetry. Authors use alliteration in stories to help words flow. Alliteration is also fun to use in dialogue when characters are being funny or playful.

Read and Find On page 8, Salesi is reflecting on the time he has spent in L.A. and how different it is from home: "Salesi thought he was on another, very peculiar planet." Here, alliteration of *peculiar* and *planet* helps to connect the words. On page 10, Salesi sees the TV commercial for a Pacific island vacation. He feels homesick and a "little lonely." The writer could have just written that he was *lonely*, but the alliteration with the word *little* sounds pleasing to the reader.

Your Turn

Write a menu for a picnic using alliteration. For example, you might bring "pleasing peanut butter sandwiches" or "lickable lollipops" for a final treat. Be creative with your menu. Share your marvelous menu with the class.